Excavations

U.S. Department of Labor
Elaine L. Chao, Secretary

Occupational Safety and Health Administration
John L. Henshaw, Assistant Secretary

OSHA 2226
2002 (Revised)

Contents

Introduction

Excavation and trenching are among the most hazardous construction operations. The Occupational Safety and Health Administration's (OSHA) Excavation and Trenching standard, *Title 29 of the Code of Federal Regulation (CFR)*, Part 1926.650, covers requirements for excavation and trenching operations. This booklet highlights key elements of the standard, shows ways to protect employees against cave-ins, and describes safe work practices for employees.

What is the difference between an excavation and a trench?

OSHA defines an excavation as any man-made cut, cavity, trench, or depression in the earth's surface formed by earth removal. This can include excavations for anything from cellars to highways. A trench is defined as a narrow underground excavation that is deeper than it is wide, and no wider than 15 feet (4.5 meters).

What are the dangers of trenching and excavation operations?

Trenching and excavation work presents serious hazards to all workers involved. Cave-ins pose the greatest risk and are much more likely than other excavation-related accidents to result in worker fatalities. Other potential hazards include falls, falling loads, hazardous atmospheres, and incidents involving mobile equipment.

OSHA's Excavation and Trenching Standard

What does the OSHA standard cover, and what protections does it offer?

The rule applies to all open excavations made in the earth's surface, including trenches. Strict compliance with all sections of the standard will prevent or greatly reduce the risk of cave-ins as well as other excavation-related accidents.

What kinds of excavations and trenches are not covered?

The standard does not apply to house foundation/basement excavations, including those that become trenches by definition when constructing formwork, foundations, or walls. For this exemption to apply, all the following conditions must exist:

- The excavation is less than 7-1/2 feet (2.5 meters) deep or is benched for at least 2 feet (.61 meters) horizontally for every 5 feet (1.52 meters) or less of vertical height;

- The bottom of the excavation, from the excavation face to the formwork or wall, is at least 2 feet (.61 meters) wide, and wider if possible;

- No water, surface tension cracks, or other environmental conditions reduce the excavation's stability;

- No heavy equipment is vibrating the excavation while employees are in it;

- Soil, equipment, and material surcharge loads are no closer to the top edge of the excavation than the excavation is deep. When you use front-end loaders to dig the excavations, place the soil surcharge load as far back from the edge of the excavation as possible, but never closer than 2 feet (.61 meters);

- The fewest crew members possible are performing the work; and

- Workers spend the minimum time possible in the excavation.

This exemption does not apply to utility excavations or trenches, which are covered by *29 CFR* 1926.652.

Preplanning

Why is it important to preplan the excavation work?

No matter how many trenching, shoring, and backfilling jobs you have done in the past, it is important to approach each new job with the utmost care and preparation. Many on-the-job accidents result directly from inadequate initial planning. Waiting until after the work has started to correct mistakes in shoring or sloping slows down the operation, adds to the cost, and increases the possibility of a cave-in or other excavation failure.

What safety factors should you consider when bidding on a job?

Before preparing a bid, you will want to know as much as possible about the jobsite and the materials you will need to have on hand to perform the work safely and in compliance with OSHA standards. A safety checklist may prove helpful when you consider specific site conditions such as the following:

- Traffic,
- Proximity and physical conditions of nearby structures,
- Soil,
- Surface and ground water,
- Location of the water table,
- Overhead and underground utilities, and
- Weather.

You can determine these and other conditions through jobsite studies, observations, test borings for soil type or conditions, and consultations with local officials and utility companies. This information will help you determine the amount, kind, and cost of safety equipment you will need to perform the work in the safest manner possible.

How can you avoid hitting underground utility lines and pipes during excavation work?

Before starting work, the OSHA standard requires you to do the following:

- Determine the approximate location of utility installations—sewer, telephone, fuel, electric, and water lines; or any other underground installations;

- Contact the utility companies or owners involved to inform them of the proposed work within established or customary local response times; and

- Ask the utility companies or owners to find the exact location of underground installations. If they cannot respond within 24 hours (unless the period required by state or local law is longer) or cannot find the exact location of the utility installations, you may proceed with caution.

If your excavation work exposes underground installations, OSHA regulations require you to protect, properly support, or remove them.

What should you tell workers before they start the project?

When you share the details of your safety and health program with employees, it is important to emphasize the critical role you expect them to play in keeping the jobsite safe. You may want to emphasize specific rules to help reduce the risk of on-the-job injuries. These rules may include requirements that workers

- Remove or minimize all surface obstacles at the worksite that may create a hazard,

- Wear warning vests or other reflective or high-visibility garments that you provide when they are exposed to vehicular traffic,

- Wear or use prescribed protective gear and equipment correctly,

- Operate equipment only if they have been trained properly in its use and alerted to its potential hazards, and

- Follow safe work practices.

It also is important to establish and maintain a safety and health management system for the worksite that provides adequate systematic policies, procedures, and practices to protect employees from, and allow them to recognize, job-related safety and health hazards. For more information about establishing such a system, see page 18.

Protective Systems

How can you prevent cave-ins?

OSHA requires that all excavations in which employees could potentially be exposed to cave-ins be protected by

- Sloping or benching the sides of the excavation,
- Supporting the sides of the excavation, or
- Placing a shield between the side of the excavation and the work area.

How do you choose the most appropriate protective system design?

Designing a protective system can be complex because you must consider many factors: soil classification, depth of cut, water content of soil, changes due to weather and climate, or other operations in the vicinity. You are free to choose the most practical design approach for any particular circumstance. Once you have selected an approach, however, the system must meet the required performance criteria.

The OSHA standard describes methods and approaches for designing protective systems such as the following:

Method 1 — Slope the sides to an angle not steeper than 1-1/2:1; for example, for every foot of depth, the trench must be excavated back 1-1/2 feet. All simple slope excavations 20 feet (6.11 meters) or less deep should have a maximum allowable slope of 1-1/2:1. These slopes must be excavated to form configurations similar to those for Type C soil, as described in Appendix B of the standard. A slope of this gradation or less is safe for any type of soil.

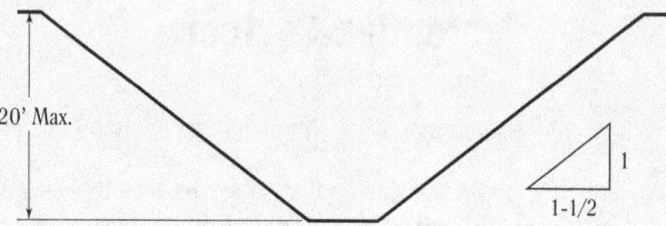

20' Max.

1

1-1/2

Figure 1. *Excavations Made in Type C Soil*

Method 2 — Use tabulated data such as tables and charts approved by a registered professional engineer to design the excavation. These data must be in writing and must include enough explanatory information, including the criteria for making a selection and the limits on the use of the data, for the user to make a selection. At least one copy of the data, including the identity of the registered professional engineer who approved it, must be kept at the worksite during construction of the protective system. After the system is completed, the data may be stored away from the jobsite, but a copy must be provided upon request to the Assistant Secretary of Labor for OSHA.

Method 3 — Use a trench box or shield designed or approved by a registered professional engineer or based on tabulated data prepared or approved by a registered professional engineer. Timber, aluminum, or other suitable materials may also be used. OSHA standards permit the use of a trench shield (also known as a welder's hut) if it provides the same level of protection or more than the appropriate shoring system.

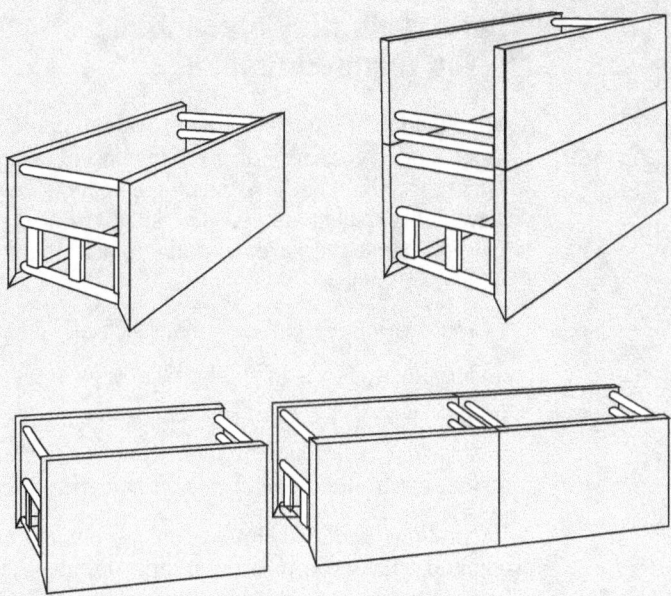

Figure 2. *Trench Shields*

Employers can choose the most practical method for the particular circumstance, but that system must meet the required performance criteria. The standard does not require a protective system when an excavation is made entirely in stable rock or is less than 5 feet (1.52 meters) deep, if a competent person has examined the ground and found no indication of a potential cave-in.

What other safety precautions are you required to take?

The standard requires you to provide support systems such as shoring, bracing, or underpinning to ensure that adjacent structures such as buildings, walls, sidewalks, or pavements remain stable. The standard also prohibits excavation below the base or footing of any foundation or retaining wall unless

- You provide a support system such as underpinning,

- The excavation is in stable rock, or

- A registered professional engineer determines that the structure is far enough away from the excavation and that excavation will not pose a hazard to employees.

Excavations under sidewalks and pavements are prohibited unless you provide an appropriately designed support system or another effective means of support.

How do you safely install and remove protective systems?

The standard requires you to take the following steps to protect employees when installing support systems:

- Connect members of support systems securely,

- Install support systems safely,

- Avoid overloading members of support systems, and

- Install other structural members to carry loads imposed on the support system when you need to remove individual members temporarily.

In addition, the standard permits excavation of 2 feet (.61 meters) or less below the bottom of the members of a support or shield system of a trench if the system is designed to resist the forces calculated for the full depth of the trench. In addition, there must be no indications, while the trench is open, of a possible cave-in below the bottom of the support system. Also, you must coordinate the installation of support systems closely with the excavation work.

As soon as work is completed, you are required to backfill the excavation when you dismantle the protective system. After the excavation is cleared, remove the protective system from the bottom up, taking care to release members slowly.

How should you maintain materials and equipment used for protective systems?

You are responsible for maintaining materials and equipment used for protective systems. Defective and damaged materials and equipment can cause failure of a protective system and other excavation hazards.

To avoid possible failure of a protective system, you must ensure that

- Materials and equipment are free from damage or defects;

- Manufactured materials and equipment are used and maintained consistent with the manufacturer's recommendations, so as to prevent employee exposure to hazards; and while in operation,

- A competent person examines any damaged materials and equipment. You must remove unsafe materials and equipment from service until a registered professional engineer evaluates and approves them for use.

Additional Hazards and Protections

What other excavation hazards do you need to protect workers against?

In addition to cave-ins and related hazards, workers involved in excavation work also are exposed to hazards involving falls, falling loads, and mobile equipment. To protect employees from these hazards, OSHA requires you to take the following precautions:

- Keep materials or equipment that might fall or roll into an excavation at least 2 feet (.61 meters) from the edge of excavations, or use retaining devices, or both.

- Provide warning systems such as mobile equipment, barricades, hand or mechanical signals, or stop logs to alert operators to the edge of an excavation. If possible, keep the grade away from the excavation.

- Provide scaling to remove loose rock or soil, or install protective barricades and other equivalent protection to protect employees against falling rock, soil, or materials.

- Prohibit employees from working on faces of sloped or benched excavations at levels above other employees unless you provide the employees at the lower levels adequate protection from the hazard of falling, rolling, or sliding material or equipment.

- Prohibit employees from standing or working under loads being handled by lifting or digging equipment. Require workers to stand away from vehicles being loaded or unloaded to protect them from being struck by any spillage or falling materials. You may permit operators to remain inside cabs of vehicles if they provide adequate protection from falling loads during loading and unloading operations.

What is the effect of water accumulation on excavation safety?

Among the additional hazards stemming from water in an excavation are undermining the sides and making it more difficult to get out of the excavation. The OSHA standard prohibits employees from working without adequate protection in excavations where water has accumulated or is accumulating. If you use water removal equipment to control or prevent water accumulation, you must ensure that a competent person monitors the equipment and its operation to ensure proper use. OSHA standards also require the use of diversion ditches, dikes, or other suitable means to prevent surface water from entering an excavation and to provide adequate drainage of the adjacent area. In addition, a competent person must inspect excavations subject to runoffs from heavy rains.

How can you protect workers against hazardous atmospheres inside excavations?

A competent person must test any excavation deeper than 4 feet (1.22 meters) or where an oxygen deficiency or a hazardous atmosphere is present or could reasonably be expected, such as a landfill or where hazardous substances are stored nearby, before an employee enters it. If there are any hazardous conditions, you must provide the employee controls such as proper respiratory protection or ventilation. In addition, you are responsible for regularly testing all controls used to reduce atmospheric contaminants to acceptable levels.

If unhealthful atmospheric conditions exist or develop in an excavation, you must provide emergency rescue equipment such as a breathing apparatus, safety harness and line, and basket stretcher and ensure that it is readily available. This equipment must be attended when in use.

What means of access and egress are you required to provide?

OSHA requires you to provide safe access and egress to all excavations, including ladders, steps, ramps, or other safe means of exit for employees working in trench excavations 4 feet (1.22 meters) or deeper. These devices must be located in the excavation within 25 feet (7.62 meters) of all workers.

Any structural ramps you use in your operation must be designed by a competent person if they are used for employee access or egress, or by a competent person qualified in structural design if they are used for vehicles. Also, structural members used for ramps or runways must be uniform in thickness and joined in a manner to prevent tripping or displacement.

What protective equipment are employees in pier holes and confined footing excavations required to use?

An employee who enters a bell-bottom pier hole or similar deep and confined footing excavation must wear a harness with a lifeline. The lifeline must be attached securely to the harness and must be separate from any line used to handle materials. Also, while the employee wearing the lifeline is in the excavation, an observer must be on hand to ensure that the lifeline is working properly and maintain communication with the employee.

When should you conduct a site inspection?

The standard requires that a competent person inspect an excavation and the areas around it daily for possible cave-ins, failures of protective systems and equipment, hazardous atmospheres, or other hazardous conditions. Inspections also are required after natural events such as heavy rains or manmade events such as blasting that may increase the potential for hazards. If the inspector finds any unsafe conditions during an inspection, you must clear employees from the hazardous area until you take safety precautions.

The standard also requires that a competent person inspect excavations and the adjacent areas daily for possible cave-ins, failures of protective systems and equipment, hazardous atmospheres, and other hazardous conditions. If the competent person finds these conditions, all exposed employees must leave the hazardous area until necessary safety precautions are taken.

Larger and more complex operations should have a full-time safety official who makes recommendations to improve implementation of the safety plan. In a smaller operation, the safety official may be part-time and usually will be a supervisor.

Supervisors are the contractor's representatives on the job. Supervisors should conduct inspections, investigate accidents, and anticipate hazards. They should ensure that employees receive on-the-job safety and health training. They also should review and strengthen overall safety and health precautions to guard against potential hazards, get the necessary worker cooperation in safety matters, and make frequent reports to the contractor.

OSHA Assistance, Services, and Programs

How can OSHA help me?

OSHA can provide extensive help through a variety of programs, including assistance about safety and health programs, state plans, workplace consultations, Voluntary Protection Programs, strategic partnerships, training and education, and more.

How does safety and health program management help employers and employees?

Effective management of worker safety and health protection is a decisive factor in reducing the extent and severity of work-related injuries and illnesses and their related costs. In fact, an effective safety and health management system forms the basis of good worker protection and can save time and money—about $4 for every dollar spent—and increase productivity.

To assist employers and employees in developing effective safety and health programs, OSHA published recommended *Safety and Health Program Management Guidelines* (*Federal Register* 54(18):3904–3916, January 26, 1989). These voluntary guidelines can be applied to all worksites covered by OSHA.

The guidelines identify four general elements critical to the development of a successful safety and health management program:

- Management leadership and employee participation,
- Worksite analysis,
- Hazard prevention and control, and
- Safety and health training.

The guidelines recommend specific actions under each of these general elements to achieve an effective safety and health program. The *Federal Register* notice is available online at *www.osha.gov*.

What are state plans?

State plans are OSHA-approved job safety and health programs operated by individual states or territories instead of Federal OSHA. The *Occupational Safety and Health Act of 1970 (OSH Act)* encourages states to develop and operate their own job safety and health plans and permits state enforcement of OSHA standards if the state has an approved plan. Once OSHA approves a state plan, it funds 50 percent of the program's operating costs. State plans must provide standards and enforcement programs, as well as voluntary compliance activities, that are at least as effective as those of Federal OSHA.

There are 26 state plans: 23 cover both private and public (state and local government) employment, and 3 (Connecticut, New Jersey, and New York) cover only the public sector. For more information on state plans, see the listing at the end of this publication, or visit OSHA's website at *www.osha.gov*.

How can consultation assistance help employers?

In addition to helping employers identify and correct specific hazards, OSHA's consultation service provides free, onsite assistance in developing and implementing effective workplace safety and health management systems that emphasize the prevention of worker injuries and illnesses.

Comprehensive consultation assistance provided by OSHA includes a hazard survey of the worksite and an appraisal of all aspects of the employer's existing safety and health management system. In addition, the service offers assistance to employers in developing and implementing an effective safety and health management system. Employers also may receive training and education services, as well as limited assistance away from the worksite.

Who can get consultation assistance and what does it cost?

Consultation assistance is available to small employers (with fewer than 250 employees at a fixed site and no more than 500 corporatewide) who want help in establishing and maintaining a safe and healthful workplace.

Funded largely by OSHA, the service is provided at no cost to the employer. Primarily developed for smaller employers with more hazardous operations, the consultation service is delivered by state governments employing professional safety and health consultants. No penalties are proposed or citations issued for hazards identified by the consultant. The employer's only obligation is to correct all identified serious hazards within the agreed-upon correction time frame.

Can OSHA assure privacy to an employer who asks for consultation assistance?

OSHA provides consultation assistance to the employer with the assurance that his or her name and firm and any information about the workplace will not be routinely reported to OSHA enforcement staff.

Can an employer be cited for violations after receiving consultation assistance?

If an employer fails to eliminate or control a serious hazard within the agreed-upon time frame, the consultation project manager must refer the situation to the OSHA enforcement office for appropriate action. This is a rare occurrence, however, since employers request the service for the expressed purpose of identifying and fixing hazards in their workplaces.

Does OSHA provide any incentives for seeking consultation assistance?

Yes. Under the consultation program, certain exemplary employers may request participation in OSHA's Safety and Health Achievement Recognition Program (SHARP). Eligibility for participation in SHARP includes, but is not limited to, receiving a full-service, comprehensive consultation visit, correcting all identified hazards, and developing an effective safety and health management system.

Employers accepted into SHARP may receive an exemption from programmed inspections (not complaint or accident investigation inspections) for a period of 1 year initially, or 2 years upon renewal. For more information concerning consultation assistance, see the list of consultation offices beginning on page 42, contact your regional or area OSHA office, or visit OSHA's website at *www.osha.gov*.

What are the Voluntary Protection Programs?

Voluntary Protection Programs (VPPs) represent one part of OSHA's effort to extend worker protection beyond the minimum required by OSHA standards. VPP—along with onsite consultation services, full-service area offices, and OSHA's Strategic Partnership Program (OSPP)— represents a cooperative approach which, when coupled with an effective enforcement program, expands worker protection to help meet the goals of the *OSH Act*.

How do the VPP work?

There are three levels of VPPs: Star, Merit, and Demonstration. All are designed to do the following:

- Recognize employers who have successfully developed and implemented effective and comprehensive safety and health management systems;

- Encourage these employers to continuously improve their safety and health management systems;

- Motivate other employers to achieve excellent safety and health results in the same outstanding way; and

- Establish a relationship between employers, employees, and OSHA that is based on cooperation.

How do VPP help employers and employees?

VPP participation can mean the following:

- Fewer worker fatalities, injuries, and illnesses;

- Lost-workday case rates generally 50 percent below industry averages;

- Lower workers' compensation and other injury- and illness-related costs;

- Improved employee motivation to work safely, leading to a better quality of life at work;

- Positive community recognition and interaction;

- Further improvement and revitalization of already-good safety and health programs; and a

- Positive relationship with OSHA.

How does OSHA monitor VPP sites?

OSHA reviews an employer's VPP application and conducts a VPP Onsite Evaluation to verify that the safety and health management systems described are operating effectively at the site. OSHA conducts onsite evaluations on a regular basis, annually for participants at the Demonstration level, every 18 months for Merit, and every 3 to 5 years for Star. Each February, all participants must send a copy of their most recent annual evaluation to their OSHA regional office. This evaluation must include the worksite's record of injuries and illnesses for the past year.

Can OSHA inspect an employer who is participating in the VPP?

Sites participating in VPP are not scheduled for regular, programmed inspections. OSHA handles any employee complaints, serious accidents, or significant chemical releases that may occur at VPP sites according to routine enforcement procedures.

Additional information on VPP is available from OSHA national, regional, and area offices, listed beginning on page 31. Also, see **Outreach** on OSHA's website at *www.osha.gov*.

How can a partnership with OSHA improve worker safety and health?

OSHA has learned firsthand that voluntary, cooperative partnerships with employers, employees, and unions can be a useful alternative to traditional enforcement and an effective way to reduce worker deaths, injuries, and illnesses. This is especially true when a partnership leads to the development and implementation of a comprehensive workplace safety and health management system.

What is OSHA's Strategic Partnership Program (OSPP)?

OSHA Strategic Partnerships are alliances among labor, management, and government to foster improvements in workplace safety and health. These partnerships are voluntary, cooperative relationships between OSHA, employers, employee representatives, and others such as trade unions, trade and professional associations, universities, and other government agencies. OSPPs are the newest of OSHA's cooperative programs.

What do OSPPs do?

These partnerships encourage, assist, and recognize the efforts of the partners to eliminate serious workplace hazards and achieve a high level of worker safety and health. Whereas OSHA's Consultation Program and VPP entail one-on-one relationships between OSHA and individual worksites, most strategic partnerships seek to have a broader impact by building cooperative relationships with groups of employers and employees.

What are the different kinds of OSPPs?

There are two major types:

- Comprehensive, which focus on establishing comprehensive safety and health management systems at partnering worksites; and

- Limited, which help identify and eliminate hazards associated with worker deaths, injuries, and illnesses, or have goals other than establishing comprehensive worksite safety and health programs.

OSHA is interested in creating new OSPPs at the national, regional, and local levels. OSHA also has found limited partnerships to be valuable. Limited partnerships might address the elimination or control of a specific industry hazard.

What are the benefits of participation in the OSPP?

Like VPP, OSPP can mean the following:

- Fewer worker fatalities, injuries, and illnesses;

- Lower workers' compensation and other injury- and illness-related costs;

- Improved employee motivation to work safely, leading to a better quality of life at work and enhanced productivity;

- Positive community recognition and interaction;

- Development of or improvement in safety and health management systems; and

- Positive interaction with OSHA.

For more information about this program, contact your nearest OSHA office or go to the agency website at *www.osha.gov.*

Does OSHA have occupational safety and health training for employers and employees?

The OSHA Training Institute in Des Plaines, IL, provides basic and advanced training and education in safety and health for federal and state compliance officers, state consultants, other federal agency personnel, and private-sector employers, employees, and their representatives.

Institute courses cover diverse safety and health topics including electrical hazards, machine guarding, personal protective equipment, ventilation, and ergonomics. The facility includes classrooms, laboratories, a library, and an audiovisual unit. The laboratories contain various demonstrations and equipment, such as power presses, woodworking and welding shops, a complete industrial ventilation unit, and a sound demonstration laboratory. More than 57 courses dealing with subjects such as safety and health in the construction industry and methods of compliance with OSHA standards are available for personnel in the private sector.

In addition, OSHA's 73 area offices are full-service centers offering a variety of informational services such as personnel for speaking engagements, publications, audiovisual aids on workplace hazards, and technical advice.

For more information on grants, training, and education, write: OSHA Training Institute, Office of Training and Education, 1555 Times Drive, Des Plaines, IL 60018; call (847) 297–4810; or see **Outreach** on OSHA's website at *www.osha.gov*.

Does OSHA give money to organizations for training and education?

OSHA awards grants through its Susan Harwood Training Grant Program to nonprofit organizations to provide safety and health training and education to employers and workers in the workplace. The grants focus on programs that will educate workers and employers in small business (fewer than 250 employees), training workers and employers about new OSHA standards or about high-risk activities or hazards. Grants are awarded for 1 year and may be renewed for an additional 12 months depending on whether the grantee has performed satisfactorily.

OSHA expects each organization awarded a grant to develop a training and/or education program that addresses a safety and health topic named by OSHA, recruit workers and employers for the training, and conduct the training. Grantees are also expected to follow up with people who have been trained to find out what changes were made to reduce the hazards in their workplaces as a result of the training.

Each year OSHA has a national competition that is announced in the *Federal Register* and on the Internet at www.osha-slc.gov/Training/sharwood/sharwood.html. If you do not have access to the Internet, you can contact the OSHA Office of Training and Education, 1555 Times Drive, Des Plaines, IL 60018, (847) 297–4810, for more information.

Does OSHA have other assistance materials available?

OSHA has a variety of materials and tools available on its website at *www.osha.gov*. These include eTools, Expert Advisors, Electronic Compliance Assistance Tools (e-CATs), Technical Links, regulations, directives, publications, videos, and other information for employers and employees. OSHA's software programs and compliance assistance tools walk you through challenging safety and health issues and common problems to find the best solutions for your workplace. OSHA's comprehensive publications program includes more than 100 titles to help you understand OSHA requirements and programs.

OSHA's CD-ROM includes standards, interpretations, directives, and more and can be purchased on CD-ROM from the U.S. Government Printing Office. To order, write to the Superintendent of Documents, U.S. Government Printing Office, Washington, DC 20402, or phone (202) 512–1800. Specify *OSHA Regulations, Documents and Technical Information on CD-ROM (ORDT)*, GPO Order No. S/N 729-013-00000-5.

What do I do in case of an emergency or if I need to file a complaint?

To report an emergency, file a complaint, or seek OSHA advice, assistance, or products, call (800) 321–OSHA or contact your nearest OSHA regional or area office listed at the end of this publication. The teletypewriter (TTY) number is (877) 889–5627.

You can also file a complaint online and obtain more information on OSHA federal and state programs by visiting OSHA's website at *www.osha.gov*.

OSHA Regional and Area Offices

OSHA Regional Offices

Region I
(CT,* ME, MA, NH, RI, VT*)
JFK Federal Building, Room E340
Boston, MA 02203
(617) 565–9860

Region II
(NJ,* NY,* PR,* VI*)
201 Varick Street, Room 670
New York, NY 10014
(212) 337–2378

Region III
(DE, DC, MD,* PA,* VA,* WV)
The Curtis Center
170 S. Independence Mall West
Suite 740 West
Philadelphia, PA 19106-3309
(215) 861–4900

Region IV
(AL, FL, GA, KY,* MS,
NC,* SC,* TN*)
SNAF
61 Forsyth Street SW
Room 6T50
Atlanta, GA 30303
(404) 562–2300

Region V
(IL, IN,* MI,* MN,* OH, WI)
230 South Dearborn Street,
Room 3244
Chicago, IL 60604
(312) 353–2220

Region VI
(AR, LA, NM,* OK, TX)
525 Griffin Street, Room 602
Dallas, TX 75202
(214) 767–4731 or 4736 x224

Region VII
(IA,* KS, MO, NE)
City Center Square
1100 Main Street, Suite 800
Kansas City, MO 64105
(816) 426–5861

Region VIII
(CO, MT, ND, SD, UT,* WY*)
1999 Broadway, Suite 1690
PO Box 46550
Denver, CO 80202-5716
(303) 844–1600

Region IX
(American Samoa, AZ,* CA,* HI,
NV,* Northern Mariana Islands)
71 Stevenson Street, Room 420
San Francisco, CA 94105
(415) 975–4310

Region X
(AK,* ID, OR,* WA*)
1111 Third Avenue, Suite 715
Seattle, WA 98101-3212
(206) 553–5930

---

*These states and territories operate their own OSHA-approved
job safety and health programs (Connecticut, New Jersey and
New York plans cover public employees only). States with
approved programs must have a standard that is identical to,
or at least as effective as, the federal standard.

OSHA Area Offices

Anchorage, AK
(907) 271–5152

Birmingham, AL
(205) 731–1534

Mobile, AL
(334) 441–6131

Little Rock, AR
(501) 324–6291 (5818)

Phoenix, AZ
(602) 640–2348

Sacramento, CA
(916) 566–7471

San Diego, CA
(619) 557–5909

Denver, CO
(303) 844–5285

Englewood, CO
(303) 843–4500

Bridgeport, CT
(203) 579–5581

Hartford, CT
(860) 240–3152

Wilmington, DE
(302) 573–6518

Fort Lauderdale, FL
(954) 424–0242

Jacksonville, FL
(904) 232–2895

Tampa, FL
(813) 626–1177

Savannah, GA
(912) 652–4393

Smyrna, GA
(770) 984–8700

Tucker, GA
(770) 493–6644/6742/8419

Des Moines, IA
(515) 284–4794

Boise, ID
(208) 321–2960

Calumet City, IL
(708) 891–3800

Des Plaines, IL
(847) 803–4800

Fairview Heights, IL
(618) 632–8612

North Aurora, IL
(630) 896–8700

Peoria, IL
(309) 671–7033

Indianapolis, IN
(317) 226–7290

Wichita, KS
(316) 269–6644

Frankfort, KY
(502) 227–7024

Baton Rouge, LA
(225) 389–0474 (0431)

Braintree, MA
(617) 565–6924

Methuen, MA
(617) 565–8110

Springfield, MA
(413) 785–0123

Linthicum, MD
(410) 865–2055/2056

August, ME
(207) 622–8417

Bangor, ME
(207) 941–8177

Portland, ME
(207) 780–3178

Lansing, MI
(517) 327–0904

Minneapolis, MN
(612) 664–5460

Kansas City, MO
(816) 483–9531

St. Louis, MO
(314) 425–4289

Jackson, MS
(601) 965–4606

Billings, MT
(406) 247–7494

Raleigh, NC
(919) 856–4770

Bismark, ND
(701) 250–4521

Omaha, NE
(402) 221–3182

Concord, NH
(603) 225–1629

Avenel, NJ
(732) 750–3270

Hasbrouck Heights, NJ
(201) 288–1700

Marlton, NJ
(609) 757–5181

Parsippany, NJ
(973) 263–1003

Albuquerque, NM
(505) 248–5302

Carson City, NV
(775) 885–6963

Albany, NY
(518) 464–4338

Bayside, NY
(718) 279–9060

Bowmansville, NY
(716) 684–3891

New York, NY
(212) 466–2482

North Syracuse, NY
(315) 451–0808

Tarrytown, NY
(914) 524–7510

Westbury, NY
(516) 334–3344

Cincinnati, OH
(513) 841–4132

Cleveland, OH
(216) 522–3818

Columbus, OH
(614) 469–5582

Toledo, OH
(419) 259–7542

Oklahoma City, OK
(405) 231–5351 (5389)

Portland, OR
(503) 326–2251

Allentown, PA
(610) 776–0592

Erie, PA
(814) 833–5758

Harrisburg, PA
(717) 782–3902

Philadelphia, PA
(215) 597–4955

Pittsburgh, PA
(412) 395–4903

Wilkes–Barre, PA
(570) 826–6538

Guaynabo, PR
(787) 277–1560

Providence, RI
(401) 528–4669

Columbia, SC
(803) 765–5904

Nashville, TN
(615) 781–5423

Austin, TX
(512) 916–5783 (5788)

Corpus Christi, TX
(512) 888–3420

Dallas, TX
(214) 320–2400 (2558)

El Paso, TX
(915) 534–6251

Fort Worth, TX
(817) 428–2470 (485–7647)

Houston, TX
(281) 591–2438 (2787)

Houston, TX
(281) 286–0583/0584 (5922)

Lubbock, TX
(806) 472–7681 (7685)

Salt Lake City, UT
(801) 530–6901

Norfolk, VA
(757) 441–3820

Bellevue, WA
(206) 553–7520

Appleton, WI
(920) 734–4521

Eau Claire, WI
(715) 832–9019

Madison, WI
(608) 264–5388

Milwaukee, WI
(414) 297–3315

Charleston, WV
(304) 347–5937

OSHA-Approved
Safety and Health Plans

Alaska

Alaska Department of Labor
and Workforce Development

Commissioner
(907) 465–2700
FAX: (907) 465–2784

Program Director
(907) 269–4904
FAX: (907) 269–4915

Arizona

Industrial Commission
of Arizona

Director, ICA
(602) 542–4411
FAX: (602) 542–1614

Program Director
(602) 542–5795
FAX: (602) 542–1614

California

California Department of
Industrial Relations

Director
(415) 703–5050
FAX: (415) 703–5114

Chief
(415) 703–5100
FAX: (415) 703–5114

Manager, Cal/OSHA
Program Office
(415) 703–5177
FAX: (415) 703–5114

Connecticut

Connecticut Department
of Labor

Commissioner
(860) 566–5123
FAX: (860) 566–1520

Conn-OSHA Director
(860) 566–4550
FAX: (860) 566–6916

Hawaii

Hawaii Department of Labor
and Industrial Relations

Director
(808) 586–8844
FAX: (808) 586–9099

Administrator
(808) 586–9116
FAX: (808) 586–9104

Indiana

Indiana Department of Labor

Commissioner
(317) 232–2378
FAX: (317) 233–3790

Deputy Commissioner
(317) 232–3325
FAX: (317) 233–3790

31

Iowa

Iowa Division of Labor

Commissioner
(515) 281–6432
FAX: (515) 281–4698

Administrator
(515) 281–3469
FAX: (515) 281–7995

Kentucky

Kentucky Labor Cabinet
Secretary (502) 564–3070
FAX: (502) 564–5387

Federal\State Coordinator
(502) 564–3070 ext.240
FAX: (502) 564–1682

Maryland

Maryland Division of Labor
and Industry

Commissioner
(410) 767–2999
FAX: (410) 767–2300

Deputy Commissioner
(410) 767–2992
FAX: (410) 767–2003

Assistant Commissioner, MOSH
(410) 767–2215
FAX: (410) 767–2003

Michigan

Michigan Department of
Consumer and Industry Services

Director
(517) 322–1814
FAX: (517) 322–1775

Minnesota

Minnesota Department of
Labor and Industry

Commissioner
(651) 296–2342
FAX: (651) 282–5405

Assistant Commissioner
(651) 296–6529
FAX: (651) 282–5293

Administrative Director,
OSHA Management Team
(651) 282–5772
FAX: (651) 297–2527

Nevada

Nevada Division of
Industrial Relations

Administrator
(775) 687–3032
FAX: (775) 687–6305

Chief Administrative Officer
(702) 486–9044
FAX: (702) 990–0358
[Las Vegas (702) 687–5240]

New Jersey

New Jersey Department of Labor

Commissioner
(609) 292–2975
FAX: (609) 633–9271

Assistant Commissioner
(609) 292–2313
FAX: (609) 292–1314

Program Director, PEOSH
(609) 292–3923
FAX: (609) 292–4409

New Mexico

New Mexico Environment
Department

Secretary
(505) 827–2850
FAX: (505) 827–2836

Chief
(505) 827–4230
FAX: (505) 827–4422

New York

New York Department of Labor

Acting Commissioner
(518) 457–2741
FAX: (518) 457–6908

Division Director
(518) 457–3518
FAX: (518) 457–6908

North Carolina

North Carolina Department
of Labor

Commissioner
(919) 807–2900
FAX: (919) 807–2855

Deputy Commissioner,
OSH Director
(919) 807–2861
FAX: (919) 807–2855

OSH Assistant Director
(919) 807–2863
FAX: (919) 807–2856

Oregon

Oregon Occupational Safety
and Health Division

Administrator
(503) 378–3272
FAX: (503) 947–7461

Deputy Administrator for Policy
(503) 378–3272
FAX: (503) 947–7461

Deputy Administrator
for Operations
(503) 378–3272
FAX: (503) 947–7461

Puerto Rico

Puerto Rico Department of
Labor and Human Resources

Secretary
(787) 754–2119
FAX: (787) 753–9550

Assistant Secretary for
Occupational Safety and Health
(787) 756–1100,
1106 / 754–2171
FAX: (787) 767–6051

Deputy Director for
Occupational Safety and Health
(787) 756–1100/1106,
754–2188
FAX: (787) 767–6051

South Carolina

South Carolina Department of
Labor, Licensing, and Regulation

Director
(803) 896–4300
FAX: (803) 896–4393

Program Director
(803) 734–9644
FAX: (803) 734–9772

Tennessee

Tennessee Department of Labor

Commissioner
(615) 741–2582
FAX: (615) 741–5078

Acting Program Director
(615) 741–2793
FAX: (615) 741–3325

Utah

Utah Labor Commission

Commissioner
(801) 530–6901
FAX: (801) 530–7906

Administrator
(801) 530–6898
FAX: (801) 530–6390

Vermont

Vermont Department of
Labor and Industry

Commissioner
(802) 828–2288
FAX: (802) 828–2748

Project Manager
(802) 828–2765
FAX: (802) 828–2195

Virgin Islands

Virgin Islands Department
of Labor

Acting Commissioner
(340) 773–1990
FAX: (340) 773–1858

Program Director
(340) 772–1315
FAX: (340) 772–4323

Virginia

Virginia Department of Labor
and Industry

Commissioner
(804) 786–2377
FAX: (804) 371–6524

Director, Office of Legal Support
(804) 786–9873
FAX: (804) 786–8418

Washington

Washington Department of Labor
and Industries

Director
(360) 902–4200
FAX: (360) 902–4202

Assistant Director
(360) 902–5495
FAX: (360) 902–5529

Program Manager,
Federal–State Operations
(360) 902–5430
FAX: (360) 902–5529

Wyoming

Wyoming Department of
Employment

Safety Administrator
(307) 777–7786
FAX: (307) 777–3646

OSHA Onsite Consultation Offices

Alabama

(205) 348–3033
(205) 348–3049 FAX

Alaska

(907) 269–4957
(907) 269–4950 FAX

Arizona

(602) 542–1695
(602) 542–1614FAX

Arkansas

(501) 682–4522
(501) 682–4532 FAX

California

(415) 703–5270
(415) 703–4596 FAX

Colorado

(970) 491–6151
(970) 491–7778 FAX

Connecticut

(860) 566–4550
(860) 566–6916 FAX

Delaware

(302) 761–8219
(302) 761–6601 FAX

District of Columbia

(202) 576–6339
(202) 576–7579 FAX

Florida

(813) 974–9962

Georgia

(404) 894–2643
(404) 894–8275 FAX

Guam

011 (671) 475–0136
011 (671) 477–2988 FAX

Hawaii

(808) 586–9100
(808) 586–9099 FAX

Idaho

(208) 426–3283
(208) 426–4411 FAX

Illinois

(312) 814–2337
(312) 814–7238 FAX

Indiana

(317) 232–2688
(317) 232–3790 FAX

Iowa

(515) 281–7629
(515) 281–5522 FAX

Kansas

(785) 296–7476
(785) 296–1775 FAX

Kentucky

(502) 564–6895
(502) 564–6103 FAX

Louisiana

(225) 342–9601
(225) 342–5158 FAX

Maine

(207) 624–6460
(207) 624–6449 FAX

Maryland

(410) 880–4970
(301) 483–8332 FAX

Massachusetts

(617) 727–3982
(617) 727–4581 FAX

Michigan

(517) 322–1809
(517) 322–1374 FAX

Minnesota

(612) 297–2393
(612) 297–1953 FAX

Mississippi

(601) 987–3981
(601) 987–3890 FAX

Missouri

(573) 751–3403
(573) 751–3721 FAX

Montana

(406) 444–6418
(406) 444–4140 FAX

Nebraska

(402) 471–4717
(402) 471–5039 FAX

Nevada

(702) 486–9140
(702) 990–0362 FAX

New Hampshire

(603) 271–2024
(603) 271–2667 FAX

New Jersey

(609) 292–3923
(609) 292–4409 FAX

New Mexico

(505) 827–4230
(505) 827–4422 FAX

New York

(518) 457–2238
(518) 457–3454 FAX

North Carolina

(919) 807–2905
(919) 807–2902 FAX

North Dakota

(701) 328–5188
(701) 328–5200 FAX

Ohio

(800) 282–1425 or
(614) 644–2631
(614) 644–3133 FAX

Oklahoma

(405) 528–1500
(405) 528–5751 FAX

Oregon

(503) 378–3272
(503) 378–5729 FAX

Pennsylvania

(724) 357–2396
(724) 357–2385 FAX

Puerto Rico

(787) 754–2171
(787) 767–6051 FAX

Rhode Island

(401) 222–2438
(401) 222–2456 FAX

South Carolina

(803) 734–9614
(803) 734–9741 FAX

South Dakota

(605) 688–4101
(605) 688–6290 FAX

Tennessee

(615) 741–7036
(615) 532–2997 FAX

Texas

(512) 804–4640
(512) 804–4641 FAX
OSHCON Request Line:
(800) 687–7080

Utah

(801) 530–6901
(801) 530–6992 FAX

Vermont

(802) 828–2765
(802) 828–2195 FAX

Virginia

(804) 786–6359
(804) 786–8418 FAX

Virgin Islands

(340) 772–1315
(340) 772–4323 FAX

Washington

(360) 902–5638
(360) 902–5459 FAX

West Virginia

(304) 558–7890
(304) 558–9711 FAX

Wisconsin (Health)

(608) 266–8579
(608) 266–9383 FAX

Wisconsin (Safety)

(262) 523–3040
(800) 947–0553
(262) 523–3046 FAX

Wyoming

(307) 777–7786
(307) 777–3646 FAX

www.ingramcontent.com/pod-product-compliance
Lightning Source LLC
Chambersburg PA
CBHW051824170526

45167CB00005B/2148